South Korea

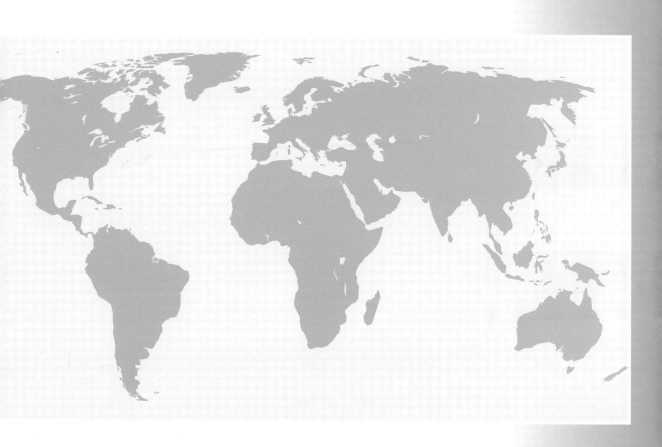

Fred Martin

Heinemann Library
Des Plaines, Illinois

© 1998 Reed Educational & Professional Publishing
Published by Heinemann Library,
an imprint of Reed Educational & Professional Publishing,
1350 East Touhy Avenue, Suite 240 West
Des Plaines, IL 60018

Designed by AMR
Illustrations by Art Construction
Printed in Hong Kong / China

02 01 00 99 98
10 9 8 7 6 5 4 3 2 1

Library of Congress Cataloging-in-Publication Data

Martin, Fred, 1948-
    South Korea / Fred Martin.
        p.   cm. — (Next stop!)
    Includes bibliographical references and index.
    Summary: Introduces the landscape, weather, plants, animals,
products, and culture of South Korea.
    ISBN 1-57572-678-5 (library binding)
    1. Korea (South)—Juvenile literature.   2. Korea (South)—
Civilization—Juvenile literature.   [1. Korea (South)]   I. Title.
II. Series.
DS902.M37   1998
915.195—DC21   97-42535
                                                         CIP
                                                          AC

Acknowledgments
The Publishers would like to thank the following for permission to reproduce photographs:
Aspect Pictures, Derek Bayes, p.25, John Earrett, p.23, Alex Langley, p.14; Colorific Photo Library,
Bill Bachman, p.6, Philip Hayson, p.26, Penny Tweedie, p.19, Barbara Wale, p.4,
David Young, p.18; J. Allan Cash, p.11; Panos Pictures, Penny Tweedie, pp.9, 27, 28; Still Pictures,
Mark Edwards, pp.15, 22, Klein/Hubert, pp.7, 8, Gerald and Margi Moss, pp.5, 10; Trip Photo
Library, R. Nichols, p.24, Eric Smith, pp.12, 13, 16, 17, 21, 29.

Cover photographs: Life File and Still Pictures

Our thanks to Betty Root for her comments in the preparation of this book.

Every effort has been made to contact holders of any material reproduced in this book.
Any omissions will be rectified in subsequent printings if notice is given to the Publisher.

Any words appearing in bold, **like this,** are explained in the Glossary.

CONTENTS

Introduction to South Korea   4

The Landscape   6

Weather, Plants, and Animals   8

Towns and Cities   10

A City Family   12

Farming and Fishing   14

A Fishing Family   16

Markets and Shops   18

South Korean Food   20

Made in South Korea   22

Transportation   24

Arts and Sports   26

Festivals and Customs   28

South Korea Factfile   30

Glossary   *31*

More Books to Read   *32*

Index   *32*

INTRODUCTION TO SOUTH KOREA

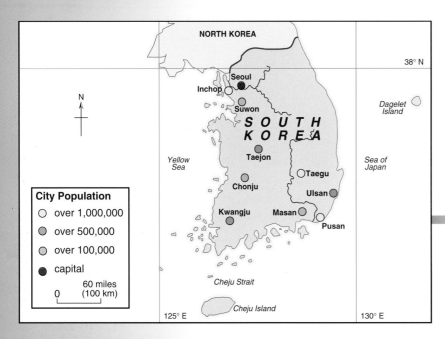

City Population
- ○ over 1,000,000
- ◐ over 500,000
- ◑ over 100,000
- ● capital

0 ⊢——⊣ 60 miles (100 km)

NORTH KOREA

38° N

Seoul
Inchon
Suwon
SOUTH KOREA
Taejon
Yellow Sea
Chonju
Taegu
Kwangju
Masan
Ulsan
Pusan
Dagelet Island
Sea of Japan
Cheju Strait
Cheju Island
125° E
130° E

South Korea: towns and population

There are old palaces and modern offices in Seoul. Seoul is the capital city of South Korea.

TWO KOREAS

South Korea and North Korea are two separate countries on the east coast of the **continent** of Asia. The people in both countries speak the same language. Korea was one country before World War II. It was divided after the war. The two countries fought each other between 1950 and 1953. They were still separate when the war ended.

4

These children are waving the South Korean flag. The divided circle on the flag is an ancient symbol.

Now the area between the two countries is a **demilitarized zone**, where soldiers cannot go. This is to prevent another war.

GETTING RICH

Most people in South Korea used to be very poor. In the last 30 years, many of them have become richer because they have worked so hard in factories. They sell the things they make all over the world.

ONE COUNTRY

Perhaps the two countries will become one country again, though it does not seem likely at the moment.

The flag of South Korea shows a circle that is divided in two parts. One side is called yin and the other side is called yang. This is an ancient sign that shows how things can be equal as well as opposite.

THE LANDSCAPE

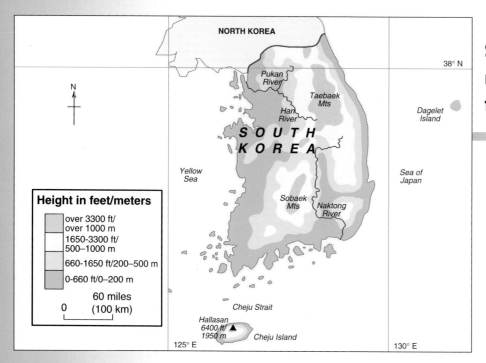

South Korea: natural features

THE PENINSULA

South Korea is on a long narrow piece of land called a **peninsula**. It is surrounded by seas on three sides. There are thousands of small islands along the coast. On Cheju, which is the largest island, there is an old **volcano**.

These children are sitting by a fast-flowing mountain stream in the Sorak Mountains.

THE MOUNTAINS

Most of South Korea is covered with mountains. Most of them are about 5,000 feet (1,500 meters) high. Some of the mountains along the coast form cliffs that go down into the sea. The highest mountain in South Korea is an old volcano called Hallasan.

The South Koreans call their own country Han.

RIVERS AND LOWLANDS

The river Han is the longest river. Most of the low flat land is in the valleys between the mountains or near the sea.

UNSAFE

South Korea is on a part of the Earth where there are **earthquakes**. The most serious earthquakes are in the south.

The tide goes out a long way along the west coast of South Korea. There are many rocky islands along this coast.

WEATHER, PLANTS, AND ANIMALS

SEASONS

Winter in South Korea is very cold. The temperature in December is below freezing almost everywhere. In summer it is warm and wet.

In winter, very cold, dry winds blow down from the center of Asia. In summer, the winds are warm and wet because they blow over a warm ocean. These are **monsoon winds**.

PLANTS

Just over half of South Korea is covered by forests. There are **coniferous** and **deciduous** forests. Some areas have been made into **national parks**. This is to protect the natural landscape.

Rivers and lakes are frozen over in winter. Standing on the ice would be very dangerous if the ice was not so thick.

There are some deciduous forests on the mountains where it is too high and too steep for farming. Coniferous trees grow where it is coldest.

ANIMALS

There are not many deer or other big animals left living in the wild in South Korea. There are many smaller animals, such as shrews, and birds including woodpeckers.

About half of all the rain in Seoul falls in June and July.

TOWNS AND CITIES

THE CAPITAL CITY

There have been cities in South Korea for at least 1,000 years. The ancient rulers built palaces, temples, and tombs in these cities. Some of these buildings are still there. Seoul is the **capital city** of South Korea. It was chosen as the capital city about 550 years ago. Some buildings in the city are very old. The Kyongbok Palace was built in 1395.

Seoul is lit up at night by lights from shops, offices, and cars. There are mountains on three sides of the city.

MODERN SEOUL

Most buildings in Seoul are modern **high-rise** office buildings, shops, factories, and apartments. The tallest building is 63 floors high. Some roads are on stilts. There is a subway system called a **metro**.

OTHER CITIES

There are about 40 big cities in South Korea. Pusan, on the south coast, is the country's biggest sea port. New factories have been built in many of the cities. The cities have grown quickly because people have come to work in the cities' offices and factories.

Seoul is almost completely surrounded by mountains. South Koreans believe that this is the best kind of place to build a city.

A CITY FAMILY

THE SHIN FAMILY HOME

The Shin family lives on the edge of the city of Seoul. Mr. and Mrs. Shin have two boys. Yongsu is eleven years old and Yongsok is eight. They live on the fourth floor of a tall apartment building.

THE DAY'S WORK

Mr. Shin works for a company that makes cars. He usually goes to work by car. He leaves at 6:30A.M. and gets home late. Mrs. Shin helps in an old people's home. She also cooks and cleans for her family.

The apartments where the Shin family live

Mr. Shin works in an office in the center of Seoul. He uses computers to help do his work.

Mrs. Shin and her two sons in a local supermarket

THE CHILDREN'S DAY

The two boys go to the same school. Many of the classes have 40 children in them. After school, the boys go home and do their homework. When they play, they enjoy meeting their friends for ball games or they go roller-skating. After dinner, they watch television or play board games.

Yongsu in his art class at school

The Shin family sit at a low table for their evening meal.

FARMING AND FISHING

CROPS AND ANIMALS

There is not much flat land for farming in South Korea. Most farms are very small. Farmers grow rice, corn, soybeans, cabbage, peppers, melons, and different types of fruit. Some keep pigs, cattle, and chickens. They also keep silk worms for their fine threads of silk.

Some farmers still use animals to do the plowing.

GROWING RICE

Rice is the main crop in South Korea. Rice grows where the weather is warm and wet. The rice fields have to be flooded with water. Rice fields are called **paddy fields**. Low mud walls around the fields keep the water in.

FISHING

Fishing is very important because there is so little land for farming. People catch squid, tuna, and most other types of fish. Some fishing boats travel thousands of miles to their **fishing grounds**.

About thirty years ago, about half the people worked in farming. Now there are not nearly as many. This is because there are better paid jobs in offices and factories.

Some fishing boats tied up in a fishing port. South Koreans eat many types of fish such as squid and tuna.

A FISHING FAMILY

The Han family outside their home

Mrs. Han waves goodbye to Mr. Han as he sets sail

THE HAN FAMILY

Han Yong-san is a fisherman. He lives with his wife Ok-hee in a small fishing village. They have a son named Yong-ho who is fifteen years old. The meanings of people's names are important in South Korea. Yong-ho means someone who stands tall and is strong.

A DAY AT SEA

On most days, Mr. Han goes out to sea on his fishing boat. He leaves in the afternoon and does not come back until the next morning. He sells the fish at a local market as soon as he gets back. Then he goes home to have breakfast. Sometimes Mrs. Han cooks a meal of boiled flatfish with red pepper.

Mrs. Han buying food

Mrs. Han cooks breakfast.

AT SCHOOL WITH YONG-HO

Yong-ho goes to school in the village. He likes learning English and math. He is good at the **martial arts** sport of *tae kwon do*. He wants to join the police when he graduates from school.

Yong-ho in his bedroom

MARKETS AND SHOPS

This scene is inside a department store in Seoul.

LIVING IN CITIES

More than half the people in South Korea live in cities. They buy what they need in shops and in street markets. They can afford to buy the best food and clothes. They also earn enough to buy television sets, computers, and other electronic goods.

A street market in Seoul. There are many markets like this in the cities.

MARKETS

Early every morning, the farmers send their food to big markets in the cities. Shop and restaurant owners buy the food there to sell to their customers.

CITY SHOPPING

The biggest and most expensive shops are in Seoul and the other cities. There are department stores and shops in modern shopping malls. Some people still like to visit street markets. There they can buy television sets, clothes, and almost anything else. Some of the goods in markets come straight from factories. They are cheaper than in the shops.

The Namdaemun market in Seoul is one of the biggest markets in the city.

SOUTH KOREAN FOOD

COOKING RICE

Rice is part of most meals in South Korea. It is boiled or fried, either on its own or mixed with eggs, vegetables, or pieces of fish.

Different types of food are cooked and sold in street markets.

SPICY FOOD

People in South Korea eat many kinds of vegetables. One favorite meal is *kimchi*. It is made from cabbage with peppers and garlic. Spices with strong, hot flavors, like ginger, are added to many cooked meals. Meat is usually cut into small chunks or strips. It is either fried in an open pan or grilled over a barbecue. One barbecued meal with meat is called *pulgogi* which means "fire dish."

EATING RULES

All the different foods cooked for one meal are put on the table together. They can be eaten in any order. People use spoons for soup, but usually eat everything else with chopsticks. Everyone waits until the oldest person starts to eat. Nobody leaves the meal until the oldest person has finished.

Young people sometimes go to McDonalds or to pizza restaurants for meals.

Meals are often eaten from a low table. People sit with legs crossed on the floor.

MADE IN SOUTH KOREA

FAMOUS NAMES

You may have something in your home that was made in South Korea. Samsung is a South Korean company that makes electronic goods, such as televisions and computers. Daewoo and Hyundai make cars.

Making cars using robots. Cars from South Korea are sold in many countries.

TOP TEN

South Korea has only made modern goods to sell to other countries for the past 30 years. Now it is in the world's top ten countries for making ships, cars, and tires. Clothes, chemicals, and most other types of goods are also made in South Korea.

SOLD ABROAD

At first, the people in factories worked hard for low wages. The products were bought by people in other countries. This brought money into South Korea and helped to make the country more wealthy. Workers now earn more and are better off.

One busy company in South Korea has built one new ship every three weeks for the last fifteen years.

Making television sets in a factory. Why do you think the worker is wearing gloves?

TRANSPORTATION

ROADS AND TRAINS

There is every kind of modern transportation in South Korea. There are highways and other main roads called expressways. These go between all the main towns and cities. There are trains for passengers and **freight**. Trains are a good way to carry heavy goods, like cars. There are high-speed trains between the biggest cities.

There are many different ways to get around in the cities.

Many people travel to work by train. This is an electric train.

AIRPORTS

The country's main airport is in Seoul. It is called Kimpo airport. Some flights are to and from other countries. Others are flights between cities in South Korea. South Korea needs a new airport because so many people want to travel by airplane.

FERRY BOATS

People can go by ferry along the coast or to the islands. The fastest journey by sea is in a special type of boat called a hydrofoil. Most of the rivers are not deep enough for boats. Factory goods are taken by ships to other countries.

An aircraft takes off or lands every two minutes at Seoul's Kimpo airport.

ARTS AND SPORTS

ANCIENT ARTS

South Korea has an ancient history of music, dancing, and poetry. The people loved to perform these in the palaces and in the villages. Many people liked to do beautiful handwriting using a brush. This is called **calligraphy**. It is now becoming a popular hobby for people in South Korea.

This choir and orchestra play music from the ancient courts and palaces.

MUSIC AND DANCE

Traditional South Korean music is made with gongs, drums, and stringed instruments. Dancers wear masks or colorful costumes. They dance slowly, sometimes balancing on one foot.

FIGHTING SPORTS

South Korea has its own form of **martial arts**, called *tae kwon do*. Many South Koreans enjoy watching and playing soccer, basketball, and baseball.

The soccer World Cup will be held in South Korea and Japan in 2002. Matches will be played in both countries.

Tae kwon do is a fighting sport from South Korea. The word tae kwon do means foot, fist, and way.

FESTIVALS AND CUSTOMS

WAYS OF CONFUCIUS

Confucius was a famous Chinese teacher who lived about 2,500 years ago. Many people in South Korea still try to follow his teaching. He said that young people must always obey older people and that everyone must obey their rulers.

These men are taking part in a Confucian ceremony.

There are many old village dances and other performances. They celebrate weddings and special times for farming.

LOCAL FESTIVALS

There are many village festivals. One is a tug-of-war between different villages. Another is a battle between monsters made by the villagers. The winning team has good luck and a good harvest.

MOONS AND MONTHS

Dates used to be figured out by the positions of the moon. Most festivals are still held at special positions of the moon. The harvest celebrations are always held on the fifteenth day of the eighth moon.

The main religions in South Korea are Buddhism and Christianity.

A PROUD PAST

South Koreans are very proud of their ancient festivals and customs.

SOUTH KOREA FACTFILE

150
◉ 대한민국 KOREA 1997

People

People from South Korea are called South Koreans.

Capital city

The **capital city** of South Korea is Seoul.

Largest cities

Seoul is the largest city, with nearly eight-and-a-half million people. The second largest city is Pusan and Taegu is the third largest city.

Head of country

South Korea is ruled by a president and a **government**.

Population

There are over 200 million people living in South Korea.

Money

The money in South Korea is called the won (W).

Language

The language spoken in South Korea is Korean.

Religion

Most people in South Korea are Buddhist or Christian and a few are Confucianist.

GLOSSARY

calligraphy a special kind of writing using a brush and ink

capital city the city where a country has its **government**

coniferous trees that have cones, such as pine trees

continent a very large area of land, usually made up of several countries

deciduous broad-leaved trees that lose their leaves in winter, such as maple trees

demilitarized zone an area between two countries where soldiers are not allowed to go so that there cannot be any fighting

earthquake a violent shaking of the ground caused by movements in the layers of the earth

fishing grounds areas where there are fish

freight goods that are moved from one place to another

government people who run a country

high-rise buildings that are very high and straight, with many floors or stories

martial arts sports where people learn how to defend themselves

metro an underground subway

monsoon winds winds that blow from different directions at different times of the year

national parks large areas where the landscape and wildlife are protected

paddy fields fields that are flooded with water for growing rice

peninsula a long, narrow area of land that juts out into the sea

volcano a mountain with hot rock inside that bursts out through the earth's surface

INDEX

animals 9

arts 26

capital 4, 10–11, 30–31

city 10–12, 18, 24, 30

farming 14

festivals 28–29

fishing 15–16, 31

food 13, 20–21

geography 4, 6–7, 11

goods 5, 18–19, 22–25

government 30–31

homes 12

language 30

martial arts 17, 27, 31

money 30

plants 8, 31

population 30

religions 29–30

school 13, 17

Seoul 4, 10–12, 18–19, 25

shopping 11, 13, 18–19

sports 13, 27

transportation 11, 24–25, 31

villages 16, 26

volcano 6, 31

weather 8, 31

MORE BOOKS TO READ

Koh, Frances M., *Korean Holidays & Festivals*. Minneapolis, MN: EastWest Press, 1990.

Lerner Publications, Dept. of Geography Staff, ed., *South Korea in Pictures*. Minneapolis, MN: Lerner Group, 1989.

McNair, Sylvia, *Korea*. Danbury, CT: LChildren's Press, 1986.